steampunk
chic

Jennifer & Kitty O'Neil

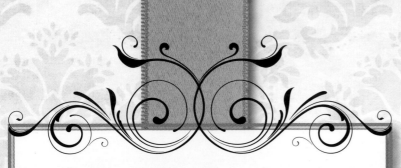

{acknowledgements}

We'd like to thank our amazing editor, Pamela Mostek, and the incredibly creative folks at All American Crafts for sharing our vision and enthusiasm for Steampunk Chic.

We'd also like to thank the generous companies who donated materials and insider know-how....AMACO, Beacon Adhesives, ETI, Jolee's, Krylon, Lisa Pavelka, Plaid, Dow Chemical, STYROFOAM, Tsukineko, Vintaj, and Walnut Hollow.

Our thanks go also to our faithful proofers, Joseph Knight and Andrew Dunne, for their brilliant comments and suggestions.

Lastly, we'd like to thank our husbands for their constant encouragement—and for loving anything and everything we create, no matter how kooky.

Published by

All American Crafts, Inc.
7 Waterloo Road
Stanhope, NJ 07874
www.allamericancrafts.com

Publisher | **Jerry Cohen**

Chief Executive Officer | **Darren Cohen**

Product Development
Director | **Brett Cohen**

Editor | **Pamela Mostek**

Proofreader | **Natalie Rhinesmith**

Art Director | **Kelly Albertson**

Product Development
Manager | **Pamela Mostek**

Every effort has been made to ensure that the information presented is accurate. Since we have no control over physical conditions, individual skills, or chosen tools and products, the publisher disclaims any liability for injuries, losses, untoward results, or any other damages which may result from the use of the information in this book. Thoroughly read the instructions for all products used to complete the projects in this book, paying particular attention to all cautions and warnings shown for that product to ensure their proper and safe use.

Printed in China
ISBN: 978-1-936708-08-6
UPC:793573035318
Library of Congress Control
Number: 2011911048

www.allamericancrafts.com

treasury of extraordinary *inventions*

steampunk
chic

What is Steampunk, you might be asking yourself. Maybe it's the first time you've seen the word, or maybe you've seen it...but didn't really know what it meant. Our own definition of steampunk is a Victorianesque restyling of everyday objects into home accents imbued with mystery and romance.

It's watch faces, keys, and gears spun together with crystals, silk, and lace, juxtaposing old and new, hard and soft, and tough and lovely. It is a rebirth of shabby chic into a retro-Machine-Age style that is elegant, funky, and infused with soul.

We imagine unique objects of beauty filled with the meaning these keepsakes carry inside. **Steampunk Chic** is the union of antique technology with Victorian charm and elegance. Crystals and lace soften the hard edges of cogs, hex nuts, and spoked washers, while keyholes, padlocks, and sepia photographs evoke romance and mystery.

We love creating in this style because we can't resist the allure of old treasures. Skeleton keys make us wonder what each one once locked and unlocked.

Hand-cancelled postage stamps sent something important through the mail, but what was it? A love letter? Broken watches stand still in time, and their intricate gears remind us of tiny jewels. Vintage accoutrements make our minds race with ideas.

In this book, we've given you the type, size, and color of all the treasures we've used to create the projects. Remember, this is just a starting point for you and your creativity. If you can't find exactly what we've used, just use what you have or look for something similar. This will make your steampunk projects uniquely yours.

When it comes to gathering steampunk finds, we love to hit every flea market, thrift store, and garage sale around. We never know what we'll discover in the bottoms of long-forgotten drawers, suitcases, and shoeboxes—or how these magic mementos will transform our projects. Go on your own adventure and put together a palette of locks, clocks, and keys to mix with beads, buttons, and ribbons. Then use your imagination to fashion your own version of steampunk chic. For more ideas, visit our blog at www.RunningWithSisters.com.

a few of our favorites

{clock faces}

While you may not run across a box of ready-to-use clock faces, you might keep an eye out for broken clocks to dismantle yourself. We've also acquired some nifty gears and cuckoo clock chain from our local clock repair shop. (Thanks, Clocksmith!)

{padlocks}

Antique padlocks have a patina of mystery and secrecy that you just can't buy at the hardware store. Pick a lock that has lost its key for a real steal!

{furniture keys}

Big old skeleton keys are a bit spendy, but smaller furniture keys (which used to come with every console and credenza) are cheap. Usually a dollar or two!

{broken jewelry}

When we see a basket of jumbled jewelry, we dive right in! We love giving new life to old pieces, like cameos, charm bracelets, and rhinestone brooches.

{postage stamps}

We think of postage stamps as miniature works of art. Collect a theme, like airplanes or insects, to feature in a project. They're sold by the lot for not a lot on eBay.

{old books}

It's fun to thumb through the pages of second-hand books. We like to clip botanical drawings, obscure scientific diagrams, and interesting phrases to use out of context. Full pages in foreign languages make handsome backgrounds!

{pocket watches}

For our purposes, old pocket watches that no longer tell time work just fine. If you spot one that's missing its clock, you can turn the case into an itty-bitty vignette.

{buttons}

A warning about vintage buttons: Once you start collecting them, it's hard to stop! We fancy them all, from Victorian perfume buttons to brass uniform buttons. Get them by the jar full.

{paper ephemera}

When we find a crate stuffed with sheet music, ticket stubs, postcards, and brochures, we can't resist. Maybe we'll discover a handwritten love letter or a photo sent to a serviceman abroad!

{watch works}

Watch movements are chock full of tiny treasures. Use tweezers to pluck out the microscopic gears, or use the whole movement for big steampunk impact.

{silk flowers}

We're fond of the aged lace, ribbons, and silk flowers that once trimmed ladies' hats and corsages. These bygone notions add romance to anything they adorn!

{luggage locks}

Luggage locks are a dime a dozen at the flea market now that suitcases have to fly unsecured. It's fun to imagine what each lock once kept safe. Classified files in an operative's briefcase? The royal jewels of an heir to the throne?

{brass stampings}

We love the look of turn-of-the-century costume jewelry, so we are thrilled that you can still buy stampings pressed from the original molds. Art nouveau corners, filigree leaves, swirling shells, and intricately detailed wings can be found at flea markets, jewelry stores, and online.

{coins & tokens}

Subway tokens and coins from far-off lands are ready-made metal embellishments. Look for special coins stamped with flowers or detailed with scalloped edges. Tokens with holes in the center are perfect for making dangles.

{old photographs}

Black-and-white photographs from the flea market are loaded with stories, even if they aren't your own. And when they're someone else's old-time snapshots, you don't have to feel bad cutting them up!

{watch faces}

You can buy all kinds of watch faces at swap meets, bead stores, and online. Layer them on cigar bands or mahjong tiles, or embellish them with washers or rhinestones.

{maps}

Colorful old travel maps are ideal for steampunk projects. They take us to places we've only dreamed of.

{chandelier crystals}

These crystals still sparkle, with or without their chandelier! Contrast them with brass hardware for the height of steampunk chic.

{giant key}

When you come across a giant key, you have to wonder what giant door it used to open!

{etcetera}

Sometimes we find something we didn't even know we needed!

fittings, trappings & accoutrements

BEAD CAPS
Bead or craft store

BICONES
Bead or craft store

BICYCLE GEARS
Bike shop

BINGO TOKENS
Flea market

BLANKS
Bead or craft store

BRASS STAMPINGS
Bead or craft store

CAP NUTS
Hardware store

DECORIVETS
Bead or craft store

DRAWER PULL PLATES
Flea market

DRAWER PULLS
Flea market

**EXTERNAL-TOOTH
LOCKING WASHERS**
Hardware store

FILIGREE ROUNDS & DROPS
Bead or craft store

**FURNITURE &
SKELETON KEYS**
Flea market

GEAR SPACERS
Bead or craft store

HEX NUTS
Hardware store

**INTERNAL-TOOTH
LOCKING WASHERS**
Hardware store

KEYHOLES
Flea market

**LUGGAGE LOCKS
& KEYS**
Flea market

METAL BUSHINGS
Hardware store

**OLD-FASHIONED
HOTEL KEYS**
Flea market

PADLOCKS
Flea market

RONDELLES
Bead or craft store

SPACERS
Bead or craft store

SPARK PLUG GAPPERS
Auto parts store

SPOKED CLOCK GEARS
Flea market

STAR-SHAPED WHEELS
Hardware store

VACUUM TUBES
Hardware store

WATCH FACES
Flea market

**WRIST WATCH
MOVEMENTS**
Flea market

inventory of implements & utensils

BEACON ADHESIVES FABRI-TAC
Craft or fabric store

BEACON ADHESIVES QUICK GRIP
Craft or hobby store

BEADALON BEAD STRINGING GLUE
Bead or craft store

CHAIN-NOSE PLIERS
Bead or craft store

EYELET TOOL & EYELETS
Craft or fabric store

FLATHEAD SCREWDRIVER
Craft or hardware store

FOAM PAINTBRUSH
Craft or hardware store

GORILLA GLUE
Craft or hardware store

HEAVY-DUTY WIRE CUTTERS
Hardware store

JEWELER'S BENCH BLOCK & HAMMER
Craft or hardware store

JOLEE'S JEWELS HOT-FIX CRYSTAL TOOL
Bead or craft store

LEATHER HOLE PUNCH
Craft or fabric store

METAL HOLE-PUNCH PLIERS
Bead or craft store

SCISSORS
Bead or craft store

WALNUT HOLLOW CREATIVE METAL BURNISHING TOOL
Craft or hardware store

WIRE CUTTERS
Craft or hardware store

X-ACTO CRAFT KNIFE
Craft or hardware store

ROUND-NOSE PLIERS
Craft or hardware store

A napkin ring inspired by vagabonds and Bohemians, this table jewelry dresses your linens for high tea on a luxury caravan. Colorful satin strands, leather straps, and chains are braided together and wrapped with copper wire. The braid is fringed with beads and keys, and forever bound with a little luggage lock. We've given you the colors we used, but choose your favorite shades to make it your own.

gypsy rendezvous

{napkin ring}

flea market finds

6 luggage keys, 1"
1 luggage lock, 1¼"

materials

✦ **36"** satin ribbon, purple, ⅛" wide (cut in half)
  36" satin ribbon, blue, ⅛" wide (cut in half)
  36" suede lace, beige, ⅛" wide (cut in half)
✦ **36"** suede lace, dark brown, ⅛" wide (cut in half)
  36" suede lace, black, ⅛" wide (cut in half)
  18" chain, brushed gold
  26-gauge copper wire
✦ **22**-gauge copper wire

beads

4 crystal bicone beads, blue, 6mm
2 crystal bicone beads, charcoal, 6mm
✦ **2** crystal bicone beads, light green, 6mm
✦ **12** faceted round beads, red, 4mm

tools & supplies

  Round-nose pliers
  Wire cutters
✦ Scissors

putting it together

1 Start by knotting all the 18" strands together at one end. Divide the strands into three sections. Braid the whole length, then tie another temporary knot at the other end.

2 Cut a 14" length of 22-gauge copper wire. At one end, make a loose wrapped loop around the lock. See the instructions on page 15 for how to make a wrapped loop.

3 Slide a blue bicone onto the wire, then wrap the wire five times around the braided strand 3" from the end. Secure by wrapping the loose end around the wire above the bicone. Trim the end. Untie the loose knot at that end.

4 Curve the braided strand into a ring. Attach the lock and wrap the strand with wire in the same way as step 2.

5 To make each beaded key dangle, cut a 3" length of 26-gauge wire. Make a wrapped loop around the key, then trim. Slide a faceted round bead, a bicone, and another faceted round bead onto the wire. Make a wrapped loop through the lock wire. Trim the end.

6 Make three key dangles for each side of the lock.

nifty gifty

For a fun and funky housewarming gift, make a set of four rings for the lucky new homeowners. Buy enough ribbons, beads, and bangles for four, but make each of them look a little different.

how to make a wrapped loop

1 Bend the end of the wire in a right angle with the chain-nose pliers.

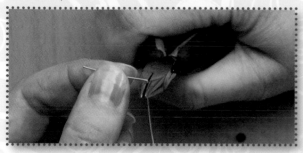

2 Twist loop into the wire with the round-nose pliers.

3 Slide a dangle onto the wire and into the loop.

4 Wrap the wire twice around the wire stem and trim the end.

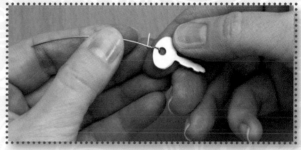

5 Slide beads onto the wire.

6 Bend the wire over the round-nose pliers and into a loop.

7 Attach the open loop to your work.

8 Wrap the end of the wire twice around the wire stem and trim the end.

curtain call

If you run across an irresistible antique padlock that is just too big for a napkin ring, consider making it into a curtain tieback. Use larger strands of fabric and ribbon and dangle furniture keys from the lock.

technique

A crystal candlestick is already dazzling on its own, but when dressed to the nines, it's as gorgeous as a bride on her wedding day. The candleholder's delicate frame is ensconced in opalescent pearls, faceted crystals, and silver-leafed keys, making it a sight to behold. A beauty as breathtaking as this has the power to light up a room even when unlit.

filigree
fascination

{candlestick}

flea market finds

- 1 crystal candlestick, 8"
- 1 crystal bobeche with 5 wire prism hangers, 3¾"
- 5 furniture keys, 1¾" to 2½"
- 6" broken rhinestone necklace
- 4 watch faces, ½"

materials

- 2 filigree open-leaf bead caps, silver and gold, 18mm
- 6 filigree open-petal flower bead caps, gold, 10mm
- 5 filigree rounds, silver, 22mm
- 4 shell connectors, brass, 18mm
- 6 round blanks, copper, ½"
- 8 jump rings, silver, 4mm
- 4 headpins, silver finish
- 48 nailhead stickers, gold, 5mm
- 66 half-pearl stickers, white, 4mm
- 1 pull-chain lamp socket, brass
- 5 hex nuts, brass, ¼"
- 6 external-tooth locking washers, ⅜"
- 1 taper candle, white
- 14-gauge copper wire
- 22-gauge antique copper wire
- 24-gauge silver-plate wire

beads

- 4 Industrial Chic chunky gear spacers, silver and gold, ⅜"
- 6 Swarovski crystal rhinestones, assorted colors, various sizes
- 42 crystal beads, assorted colors, various sizes
- 8 faceted Czech glass beads, copper, 4mm
- 4 faceted Czech glass tube beads, silver, 10mm
- 3 faceted Czech glass rondelles, amber, 7mm
- 9 pearls, 18mm
- 10 rhinestone spacers, clear/silver, 6mm
- 8 daisy spacers, silver finish, 6mm
- 4 spacers, copper, 2mm

tools & supplies

- Beadalon Bead Stringing Glue
- Clear silicone adhesive
- Silver leaf kit with silver leaf sheets, metal leaf adhesive sizing, and metal leaf sealer
- Round-nose pliers
- Chain-nose pliers
- Metal hole-punch pliers
- Wire cutters
- Paintbrush
- Hammer
- Sharpie
- Jeweler's bench block (optional)

putting it together

1 Start by embellishing the base of the candlestick with six steampunk flowers. To make each flower, layer and glue a copper disc, a locking washer, and a rhinestone. Flatten a filigree open-leaf bead cap with the hammer and glue beneath the flower as a stem.

2 Decorate the rest of the candlestick with nailhead and half-pearl stickers. Use the bead stringing glue to attach filigree bead caps, rhinestones, and the rhinestone necklace.

3 To make the copper rosette beneath the bobeche, cut a 22" piece of 14-gauge copper wire and twist eight circles approximately ½" in diameter, wrapping them around the Sharpie. Curve the looped wire into a rosette and secure by wrapping the ends of the wire together.

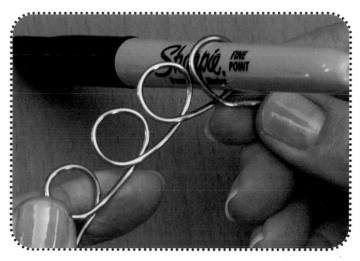

4 Make a spring by wrapping the antique copper wire around the widest end of the round-nose pliers.

5 Twist the wire around the pliers into tight loops.

6 Continue coiling the wire until you have a 1" spring. Twist a loop in each end of the spring for hanging. Make a total of four springs.

7 Punch a hole in the top of a watch face using the metal hole-punch pliers. Using the 24-gauge wire, attach the watch face to a copper spring with a wrapped loop featuring a crystal bead. Refer to page 15 for instructions to make a wrapped loop.

8 Attach the other end of the spring to a wrapped-loop component featuring a tube bead flanked by crystal beads and daisy spacers. Make a total of four watch dangles and hang them with jump rings from every other copper circle on the rosette.

9 For the rest of the rosette dangles, feed a crystal bead and a copper spacer onto a headpin and hang with a wrapped loop from the bottom of a shell connector.

10 Using the 24-gauge wire, continue on with wrapped loops connecting a crystal bead, a chunky gear, a crystal bead, a pearl, and a crystal bead. Hang the four dangles from the open loops on the rosette.

11 See page 21 for instructions on how to silver or gold leaf. Silver leaf the keys, then flatten the open-leaf bead caps with a hammer.

12 With a wrapped loop featuring alternating crystal beads and rhinestone spacers, connect the key to the open-leaf bead cap. Wire a hex nut to the open-leaf bead cap with the antique copper wire. Continue on with wrapped loops connecting a crystal bead, a filigree round, a crystal bead, a pearl, and a crystal bead with the wire hanger on the bobeche. Make a total of five key dangles.

13 Glue the crystal bobeche and the copper rosette onto the candlestick using the silicone adhesive. Let dry. Glue the lamp socket into the hole of the bobeche. Place the taper candle in the lamp socket.

how to silver or gold leaf

1 Paint the surface with metal leaf adhesive and let dry for 30 minutes.

2 Place a piece of metal leaf on the surface and rub. Continue to add pieces of metal leaf to the surface until it is covered.

3 Brush off any excess metal leaf pieces with a dry paintbrush.

4 Apply a coat of metal leaf sealant to the surface.

no-drip tip

The bobeche not only adds to the design of your candlestick, it also catches the wax drippings from the candle. You can find them at hardware stores, craft stores, and any place that sells lots of candles!

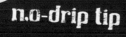

Vintage flatware sprouts from the earth, standing guard like a sterling sentinel. Extending from the knife's handle is a lone key—no lock in sight. Suspended below, a natural brass tag is embossed with the genus and species of the flora beneath. In Latin, of course.

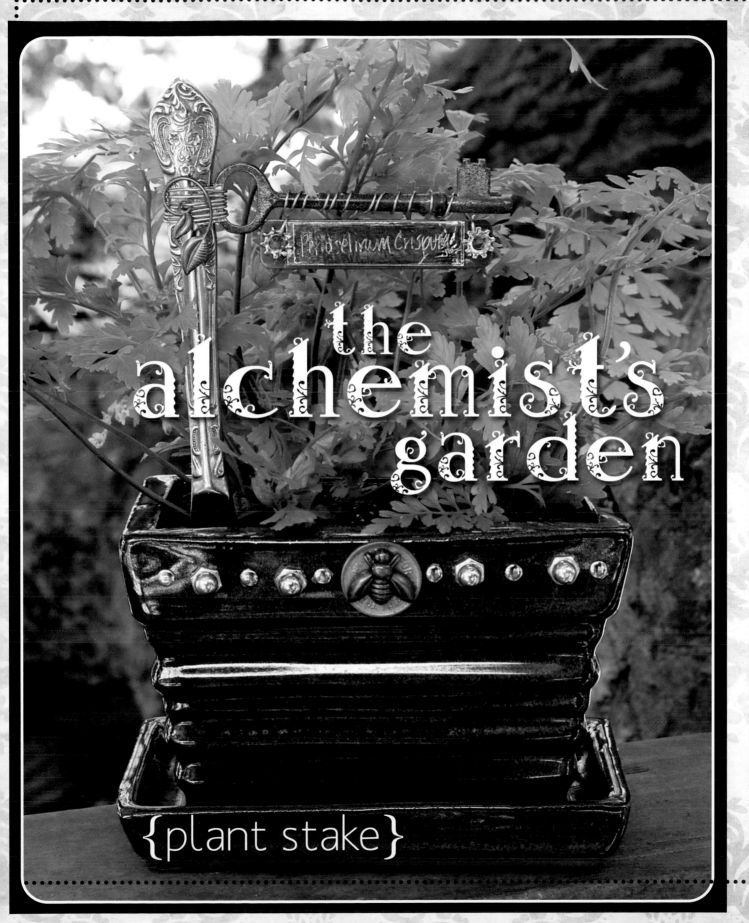

the alchemist's garden

{plant stake}

flea market finds

◆ **1** silver-plated knife
◆ **1** skeleton key, 3¼"

materials

◆ **2** external-tooth locking washers, ⅜"
◆ **1** Vintaj Leafage Fastenables, copper, 26mm
◆ **1** Vintaj Arte Metal Nameplate, 14.5mm x 68mm
◆ **20**-gauge copper wire
◆ Copper foil tape, ¼" wide
◆ Aluminum flashing tape, 2" wide

tools & supplies

◆ Beacon Adhesives Quick Grip
◆ Round-nose pliers
◆ Wire cutters
◆ Scissors
◆ Ballpoint pen

putting it together

1 Start by holding the key perpendicular to the knife handle. Tightly bind the key to the knife handle with the copper tape. Wrap the 20-gauge copper wire over the tape two times, then slide on the Leafage Fastenables metal embellishment. Continue wrapping until the tape is covered. Secure by twisting the ends together in the back so they don't show.

2 To create a hanger for the nameplate, twist a loop in the end of a 14" length of copper wire. Wrap the wire around the key a dozen times. Finish with another loop and trim the ends.

3 Glue the locking washers over the holes in the nameplate.

4 Cut a piece of aluminum tape to fit the nameplate. In handwritten script, emboss the Latin name of the plant on the tape using a ballpoint pen.

5 Center the tape on the nameplate. Hang the labeled nameplate from the two loops beneath the key.

curious conservatory

Create a steampunk windowsill garden indoors by adorning terra cotta pots with assorted hardware. As you can see in the photo on page 23, we used cap nuts, nailhead stickers, a subway token, and a bee button with the shank removed.

A book is a box containing stories, which are told and retold when opened and locked up under cover when closed. The pages inside recall a room with a key, a locket, and a handwritten note—small, but not insignificant. A story to be read and reread. How will it end?

gas lamp love story

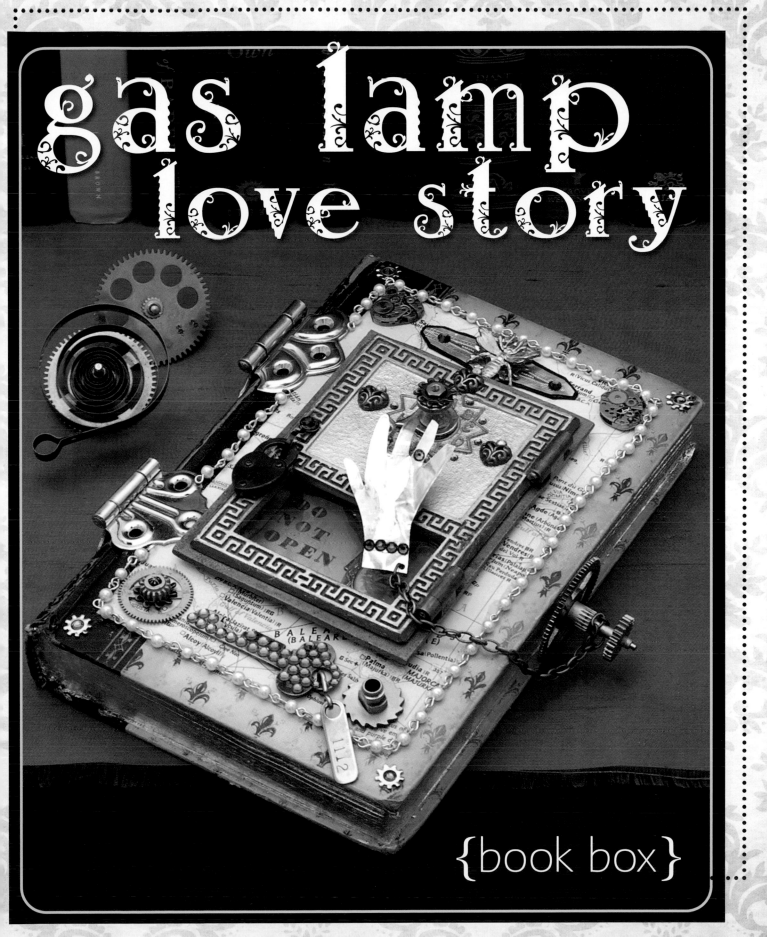

{book box}

materials

- ✦ 1 piece of black velvet, approximately 12" x 12"
- ✦ 2 decorative cabinet hinges, mixed metals
- ✦ 16" white rosary chain
- ✦ 3 heart charms, brass, ½"
- ✦ 1 bee brooch, 1"
- ✦ 1 set ¼" alphabet rubber stamps
- ✦ 5½" chain, antique gold
- ✦ 1 piece of leather, black, 1" x 2½"
- ✦ 1 machine screw nut, brass, ¼"
- ✦ 1 Industrial Chic chunky gear spacer, gold, ⅜"
- ✦ 2 Industrial Chic flat gear spacers, antique gold, ½"
- ✦ 1 external-tooth locking washer, ¾"
- ✦ 4 external-tooth locking washers, ¼"
- ✦ 1 crystal bicone, teal, 4mm
- ✦ 1 Walnut Hollow Creative Metal Square, aluminum, 40 gauge
- ✦ 26-gauge copper wire
- ✦ Rub 'n Buff, Silver Leaf
- ✦ Krylon 18KT. Gold Leafing Pen
- ✦ Gold leaf kit with gold leaf sheets, adhesive, and sealer

rhinestones

- ✦ 36 Swarovski crystal rhinestones, teal, 4mm
- ✦ 16 Swarovski crystal rhinestones, teal, 3mm
- ✦ 3 Swarovski crystal rhinestones, crystal AB, 3mm
- ✦ 2 Swarovski crystal rhinestones, topaz, 5mm
- ✦ 4 Swarovski crystal rhinestones, topaz, 4mm

flea market finds

- ✦ 1 hardback book, approximately 5¾" x 8½" x 1¼"
- ✦ 1 old map
- ✦ 1 vintage post office box door with doorframe
- ✦ 1 small heart-shaped padlock
- ✦ 1 cigar band
- ✦ 1 safe deposit box key with stamped metal tag
- ✦ 2 ladies' wrist watch movements
- ✦ 1 spoked clock gear, 1"
- ✦ 1 clock gear and axle assembly, 1½" diameter gear with 1½" long axle
- ✦ 1 ratchet wheel, ¾"
- ✦ 1 clock hand, 1½"

tools & supplies

- ✦ Mod Podge Decoupage Medium
- ✦ StazOn inkpad, Jet Black
- ✦ Beacon Adhesives Fabri-Tac
- ✦ Gorilla Super Glue
- ✦ Beadalon Bead Stringing Glue
- ✦ X-Acto craft knife
- ✦ Paintbrush
- ✦ Scissors
- ✦ Ruler
- ✦ Wire cutters
- ✦ Metal hole-punch pliers
- ✦ Rubbing alcohol
- ✦ Awl
- ✦ Tweezers

putting it together

1 Open the front cover of the book, press the pages together, and paint the outside edge of the page stack with Mod Podge. Let dry. Using the craft knife, cut a hollow in the page stack to fit the post office box door. Cut through almost to the back cover. Then cut an opening in the book cover the same size.

2 Refer to page 21 and gold leaf the outside edges. Using the Fabri-Tac glue to secure it in place, line the inside with black velvet.

3 Superglue the map to the front of the book over the opening, then cut out the opening in the map with a craft knife. Superglue the hinges onto the spine of the book. Create a border around the map by using super glue to adhere to the rosary chain.

4 Embellish the book cover with watch movements, gears, and spacers using the bead stringing glue. Glue a small locking washer topped with a 4mm teal rhinestone to each corner.

5 Open the cigar band and glue it flat to a piece of leather with Fabri-Tac, then cut the leather out in the shape of the cigar band. Glue this to the front of the book above the opening. Remove the backing from the bee brooch, glue it onto a large locking washer, and glue onto the cigar band using the bead stringing glue. Accent the sides of the band with two large topaz rhinestones.

6 Clean the glass of the post office box door with alcohol, then stamp the words "DO NOT OPEN" with the rubber stamps and the StazOn inkpad.

7 Embellish with heart charms, a large gear spacer, and the machine nut, attaching them with the bead stringing glue. Place the 3mm teal rhinestones around the combination lock dial and a crystal AB rhinestone on each heart charm.

8 Superglue the post office box doorframe into the opening on the front of the book. Paint the door with the silver Rub 'n Buff, then wipe the excess off with a paper towel. Be careful not to get the silver into the border.

9 Bend the clock hand into a door handle shape. Slide on the heart lock, then glue the handle to the side of the door. Superglue the teal bicone to the top of the handle.

10 To make the metal hand, draw a hand on the Creative Metal square. Cut the hand out with scissors.

11 Paint the cuff gold using the Krylon Gold Leafing Pen.

12 Using the tweezers and the bead stringing glue, encrust the cuff of the hand with the 4mm topaz rhinestones. Add a 4mm teal rhinestone ring.

13 Using the metal hole-punch pliers, make a hole in the cuff of the hand.

14 Poke a hole about ¼" deep in the side of the book pages with the awl and superglue in the axle of the clock gear assembly. Attach one end of the antique gold chain to the assembly and the other end to the hand by opening and closing the chain links.

unlocking the mystery

When you find a post office box door, make sure the combination is written inside. And don't forget to jot it down before you glue the door in place; otherwise your box will be locked forever!

15 Encrust the key with the remaining teal rhinestones using the bead stringing glue. Superglue the key to the front of the book.

16 Use the combination to open the post office box door. Stash love letters, lockets, and other treasured mementos in the velvet-lined box.

This electric hourglass began its journey as a Honduran humidor. With a trip across two hemispheres, around an analog dial, and onto low-voltage fuses, this grandfather clock not only carries the mantel, it marks the future as it happens—one moment at a time.

{mantel clock}

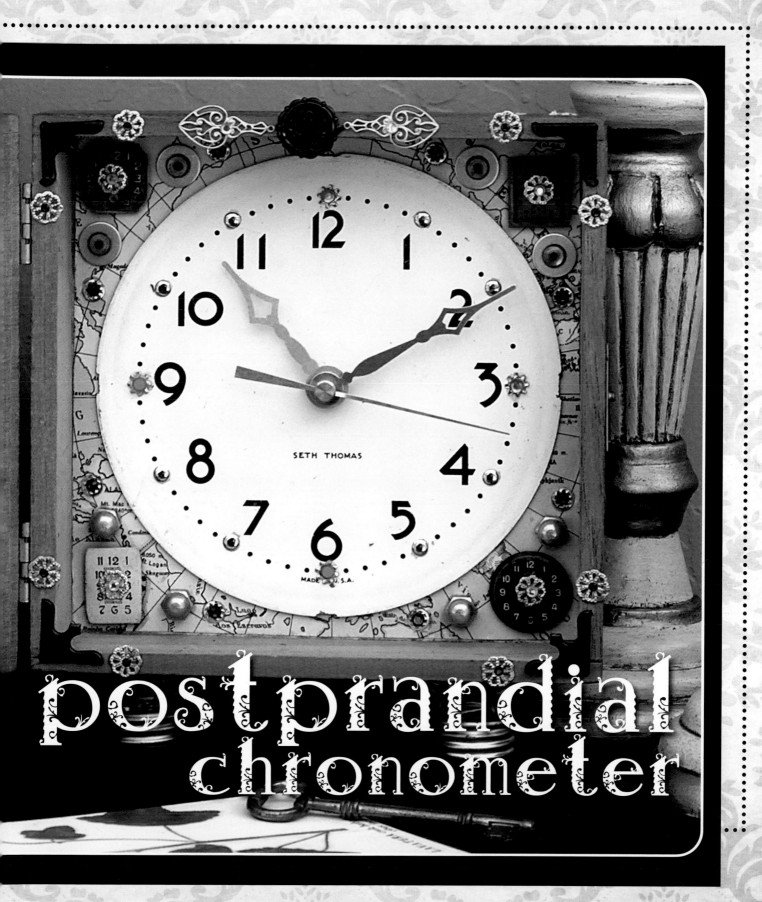

postprandial chronometer

flea market finds

1 cigar box, approximately 7" x 7" x 2¼"
1 clock face, 6"
- 4 watch faces, ¾" to 1"
- 1 old map
4 shirt buttons
- 4 plug fuses

materials

1 Walnut Hollow Clock Craft kit for ¼" thick surfaces
4 Vintaj Corner Decorivet, natural brass, 20mm
1 Vintaj Arte Metal Decorivet, Woodland Bird, 19mm
2 filigree drops, brass, 29mm
- 12 filigree bead caps, brass, 10mm
4 spacers, copper, ¼"
4 washers, brass, ½"
4 cap nuts, brass, ⅜"
4 external-tooth locking washers, ¼"
8 internal-tooth locking washers, ¼"
8 nailhead stickers, gold, 5mm
2 small nails, brass, ½"
1 AA battery

rhinestones

8 Swarovski crystal rhinestones, topaz, 2mm
8 Swarovski crystal rhinestones, topaz, 5mm
4 Swarovski crystal rhinestones, light blue, 6mm
4 Swarovski crystal rhinestones, crystal, 4mm
2 Swarovski crystal rhinestones, crystal AB, 4mm

tools & supplies

Beacon Adhesives Quick Grip
- Drill and 5⁄16" drill bit
- Hammer
- Jeweler's bench block (optional)
- Rubber cement
Ruler
- Scissors

putting it together

1 Turn the cigar box over and find the center in the back. Drill a hole 5⁄16" in diameter. Separate the clock mechanism parts, keeping them in order. Poke the battery case shaft through the hole in the cigar box from back to front.

2 Cut the map to fit inside the back of the cigar box and cut a hole to slide the clock shaft through. Use the rubber cement to glue the map in place.

3 Dot the back of the clock face with Quick Grip and slide it onto the shaft over the map. Assemble the clock mechanism following the directions on the package, sliding the hour hand, minute hand, and second hand onto the shaft.

4 Hammer the Vintaj corners to the front corners of the open cigar box. Flatten all the bead caps with a hammer on a jeweler's bench block. Glue eight hammered bead caps with topaz rhinestone centers around the edge of the open cigar box, flanking the corner rivets.

5 Using the Quick Grip, glue a shirt button to the back of each small watch face, then glue them to each corner of the map. Glue a hammered bead cap to the center of each watch face. Glue a crystal rhinestone on top.

6 Fill in the corners by flanking the watch faces with brass washers, copper spacers, locking washers, brass cap nuts, and large topaz rhinestones.

7 Glue four external-tooth locking washers to the clock face at the 12, 3, 6, and 9 o'clock positions. Glue a light blue rhinestone to the center of each locking washer. Place a nailhead sticker onto the clock face at the 1, 2, 4, 5, 7, 8, 10, and 11 o'clock positions.

8 Nail the Vintaj bird rivet to the top of the open cigar box, centering it between the corners. Nail one filigree drop to either side. Use the Quick Grip to add one crystal AB rhinestone to each nail head.

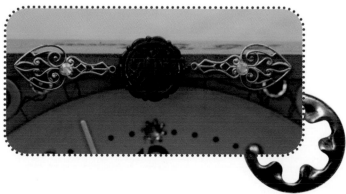

9 Use the Quick Grip to glue the plug fuses to the bottom of the cigar box and lid as feet.

10 Load the AA battery into the clock mechanism and set the time.

time stamp

Instead of using a real clock face, try making your own. Use a StazOn inkpad and number stamps to add 12, 3, 6, and 9 to a disc of acetate. Layer it over a circular saw blade and embellish with rhinestones.

Like actors from the silver screen frozen frame by frame, treasured mosaic pieces are captured for eternity. A vintage film canister presents long-lost mementos in a sea of clear resin. Trios of clock faces and skeleton keys share the starring role, while forgotten hotel keys contain a drama with mystery in its plot.

the auteur's tableau

{mosaic table}

flea market finds

1 metal film canister, approximately 15"
3 clock faces, 5½"
1 vintage keyhole
3 skeleton keys, 3" to 3½"
✦ 3 old-fashioned hotel keys, 2¾"
5 Monopoly game pieces
1 vintage bee brooch
6 uniform shank buttons
✦ 5 clock-face buttons
2 foreign coins
1 wooden bingo token
3 brass drawer pulls, 2¼"
2 metal bushings, 1"
1 bicycle gear, 2"

materials

1 brass stamping, Victorian floral fan, 54mm
1 brass stamping, flower basket, 44mm
2 alphabet cameos, black/ivory, 40mm
4 filigree drops, brass, 35mm
✦ 6 flat marbles, red, ¾"
✦ 38 flat marbles, amber, ½"
4 external-tooth locking washers, ⅜"
10 hex nuts, steel, ¾"
20 hex nuts, steel, ½"
4 hex nuts, brass, ½"
4 ft. dimpled brass chain
2 EnviroTex Lite Pour-On High Gloss Finish kits, 32 oz.

tools & supplies

✦ 16 straight-sided paper or plastic cups, 16 oz.
✦ 8 chopsticks
✦ Beacon Adhesives Glass, Metal & More
✦ Heavy-duty wire cutters
✦ Protective gloves
✦ Protective eyewear
✦ Level

putting it together

1 Take the lid off the film canister and set it aside. Center the clock faces in the canister so their edges overlap. Embellish the clock faces with the bee brooch that has pin removed, the keyhole, the bicycle gear, the bingo token, and clock-face buttons.

2 Create a border around the clock faces by alternating drawer pulls and hotel keys. Arrange flat marbles into florets. Place the cameos on either side of a hotel key like a monogram.

3 For the rest of the design, fill in the spaces with brass stampings, hardware, marbles, Monopoly pieces, and shank buttons. Lay the chain along the edge of the canister. Once you are happy with your layout, glue everything in place with the Glass, Metal & More. Let dry overnight.

4 Before you pour the first coat of the High-Gloss Finish, put on your protective gloves and eyewear. In a well-ventilated area, properly mix the resin using the Two-Cup Method described on page 39, according to the manufacturer's instructions.

5 Immediately pour the resin mixture directly over the items in the canister. Be sure resin falls across every item, keeping in mind that multiple coats will be needed. Tilt the canister to help the resin reach all areas.

6 Place the canister on a perfectly level surface in a dust-free area. Five minutes after the resin is poured, bubbles may appear. To release them, exhale over the surface of the resin. Cover the mosaic. The canister lid works great for this—just leave a gap for gas to escape. Let cure for 8 to 1o hours.

7 To create a floating layer in the mosaic, set a skeleton key on top of each clock face. Mix and pour another layer of resin and let cure.

8 If the resin is smooth and covers everything, you are done. If not, clean with alcohol and add another layer of resin.

9 Glue stainless hex nuts in a pattern around the outside edge of the canister. Glue the canister to a large wooden spool embellished with upholstery tacks or set it on a wrought-iron plant stand or even an old crate.

it's in the can.

Can't find a vintage film canister at the flea market? Try an online party store or your local party supply shop around Oscar time.

1 Pour the resin into a cup until the cup is a little less than half full.

2 Pour the same amount of hardener into a second cup.

3 Pour the hardener and the resin together into a third cup.

4 Whip the mixture with a chopstick for one minute.

5 Pour the whipped mixture into a fourth cup.

6 Whip the mixture with a new chopstick for one minute. Use immediately.

Both sweet and beguiling, a formal china plate lures with a tempting treat. The foil-embossed saucer is elevated to dessert course status, but a spoked pedestal portends hidden perils and warns this is an aperitif of danger.

the beekeeper's rostrum

{cupcake stand}

flea market finds

✦ 1 open-lace china plate, 6"
✦ 1 crystal cordial glass, 3"
✦ 8 tiny keys, 1" to 1¼"
✦ 1 bicycle gear cassette, 5½"
✦ 1 rhinestone bee brooch

materials

✦ 26 crystal beads and bicones, assorted colors, various sizes
✦ 6 Vintaj spoke charms, silver, 19mm
✦ 4 lobster clasps, antique gold, 15mm
✦ 9 Swarovski crystal rhinestones, teal, 2mm
✦ 9 external-tooth locking washers, ⅜"
✦ 20 spacers, copper, 6mm
✦ 22-gauge silver-plate wire
✦ 24-gauge silver-plate wire
✦ Lisa Pavelka Magic-Glos UV resin

tools & supplies

✦ Gorilla Super Glue
✦ Round-nose pliers
✦ Wire cutters

putting it together

1 Turn the plate upside down on a table. Place the rhinestone bee brooch inside the cordial glass. Flip the cordial glass upside down, holding the bee inside with one finger.

2 Center the cordial glass on the back of the plate, then run a bead of UV resin around the perimeter of the glass. Rock the glass around to allow the resin to seep underneath the edge. Set outside to cure in the sun for 15 minutes.

3 Flip the plate and glass over when dry, and superglue the foot of the cordial glass to the top of the bicycle gear cassette.

4 Embellish the cordial glass by wrapping the 22-gauge wire around the stem. Superglue nine locking washers around the foot of the glass. Center a rhinestone on each washer and glue into place.

5 Create eight beaded key dangles with 24-gauge wire. Make each key dangle a little different by varying the order of the beads, spoke charms, and lobster clasps.

6 Attach each dangle to the open-lace design of the plate with a beaded wrapped loop.

hang in there

If you can't find an open-face china plate, make hooks. Start with a 10mm earring blank, the kind with a flat pad on a post. Using round-nose pliers, bend the post in a loop, then superglue the pad to the underside of your plate.

get in gear

Try finding bicycle gears at the flea market or ask around at your local bike shop to see if they have any castoffs. Still no luck? Try Walmart or Sears! Just remember, you don't need a top-of-the-line 10-speed. Save your bucks and get a cheapie!

Just as a fancy dress from the Sky Captain's Ball is worn and then cast aside, this once-elegant wreath wears torn satin and faded silk flowers. Nestled within the petals of each posy, symbols of love lost: a watch face, a compass, an old photograph. A gloved hand holds a letter from across the sea—received, but never opened.

tussy mussy's corsage

{wreath}

flea market finds

- 3 clock gears, ¾" to 1"
- 3 furniture keys, 2¼" to 2½"
- 2 vintage postage stamps
- 2 pieces of old stationery
- ✦ 1 spark plug gapper
- 1 watch face
- ✦ 1 paperback romance with a dashing Casanova on the cover
- ✦ 1 bicycle gear, 2"
- 20" vintage lace
- ✦ 2 foreign coins, one with a hole in the center
- 1 compass charm
- ✦ 1 heart-shaped lock pendant

materials

- 1 STYROFOAM brand foam wreath form, 12"
- ✦ 1 TPC Studio Travel Journey Clear Stamps set, postage cancellation stamp
- 1 Andrea by Sadek hand clip, antique silver plate, 5"
- ✦ 1 picture frame pendant, brass, 2"
- 2 flower bead caps, 1¼" to 1¾"
- 4 layered silk flowers, olive green
- ✦ 1 layered silk flower, fuchsia
- 1 piece of organza, 12" x 54", coral
- 1 piece of satin, 12" x 54", coral
- 65" mesh wired ribbon, copper (cut into 2 pieces)
- 60" satin ribbon, olive, ½" wide
- ✦ 28" organza ribbon, olive, ⅛" wide
- 32" organza ribbon, raspberry, ⅛" wide
- 7 pearl-topped straight pins, fuchsia & purple
- ✦ 1 washer, zinc, ½"
- 1 washer, natural brass, 1¼"
- 1 external-tooth locking washer, ½"
- ✦ 3 external-tooth locking washers, ¼"
- ✦ 5 hex nuts, brass, ¼" to ⅜"
- ✦ 36" floral wire
- ✦ Lisa Pavelka Magic-Glos UV resin

tools & supplies

- ✦ Beacon Adhesives Quick Grip
- ✦ StazOn inkpad, Jet Black
- ✦ Scissors
- ✦ Wire cutters
- ✦ Straight pins

putting it together

1 To cover the wreath form, rip the coral satin into 2"-wide strips. Pin the end of a satin strip to the back of the wreath form and wrap the fabric around the form. Pin the end of that strip to the back and start again with a new strip. Continue in this way until the wreath is covered. Repeat with a layer of ripped organza fabric strips.

2 Wrap the raspberry ribbon three times around the left side of the wreath, slide a furniture key onto the ribbon, and tie the ends in a knot. Wrap a piece of copper ribbon three times around the upper left side of the wreath. Slide the heart pendant on and tie in a knot. Wrap another copper ribbon around the right side of the wreath, add a key, and tie the ends in a bow. Wrap the thin olive ribbon on the right side of the wreath, slide on a key, and tie the ends in a bow. Tie a scrap of lace ribbon around the wreath on the right side and tie the ends in a bow.

3 Decorate the wreath with the silk flowers by removing the center stems and separating the layers of the flowers. Remake five flowers without the stem by gluing the layers together on the wreath. Create a new center in each flower by layering a locking washer and a hex nut. Pin each flower into the wreath with a pearl-topped pin.

4 To further embellish the left side of the wreath, glue the spark plug gapper onto the wreath beside the flowers and glue a watch face on top. Finish with a small locking washer in the center. To the clock gears, add a coin with a hole in the center and pin it beneath the flowers. Pin a flower bead cap over the edge of the top flower.

5 Embellish the right side by gluing a clock gear over a large washer in the center of a bicycle gear. Layer a compass charm over a clock gear on a coin. Center that over a flower bead cap and glue onto a layer of fuchsia flowers.

6 Cut the Casanova out of the paperback romance cover and glue him into the picture frame pendant. Drip UV resin over the surface of the picture. Set outside in the sun to cure for 15 minutes. Glue onto the wreath.

7 To add the hand clip, wrap the floral wire several times around the top of the wreath and through the hole in the clip. Twist the ends to secure. Cover the wire with the wide olive satin ribbon and finish with a knot.

8 Craft a love letter out of the old stationery. Fold a second piece of paper into an envelope and slip in the love letter. Address the love letter with a florid script. Glue on two vintage postage stamps, then cancel the postage with the rubber stamp and black inkpad. Tuck the letter into the hand clip.

on the other hand

If you can't round up a hand clip, go for an old-school metal bulldog clip. You can find one at an office supply store or maybe even in your garage!

Not since the invention of the incandescent bulb has a parlor been illuminated by such an illustrious light. A hand-tinted shade embellished with flame-singed rosettes casts a provocative glow rivaled only by that of candlelight. At the heart of this lamp, a bamboo birdcage locks up tattered letters from an unrequited love.

edge of twilight

{lamp}

flea market finds

- **4** watch faces, 1"
- **8** shirt buttons, dark colors
- ✦ **4** foreign coins
- **1** bamboo birdcage, 7" x 4½" x 4½"
- **1** padlock, 2½"
- ✦ **1** organza ribbon scrap, yellow, 12"

materials

- **1** lampshade, white, 9" x 12" x 12"
- **1** bottle adapter lamp kit
- **1** piece of velvet, 8" x 54", burgundy
- **1** piece of polyester lining, 8" x 54", purple
- **1** piece of satin, 8" x 54", cranberry
- **1** piece of tulle, 8" x 54", magenta
- **37"** beaded fringe trim, black/crystal/brown
- **52"** woven ribbon trim, black
- **16** hex nuts, brass, ½"
- ✦ **16** cap nuts, zinc, ⅜"
- **4** Ballard Designs Bee Style Pins
- **4** external-tooth locking washers, ⅜"
- **4** Swarovski crystal rhinestones, blue, 5mm
- Plaid FolkArt craft paint, Cardinal Red #414
- ✦ All-purpose sewing thread, burgundy

tools & supplies

- Beacon Adhesives Fabri-Tac
- Beacon Adhesives Quick Grip
- Candle & matches
- ✦ Scissors
- ✦ Foam paintbrush
- ✦ Needle

putting it together

1 To give the lampshade an aged look, paint it inside and out with a coat of watered-down red paint. Let dry and repeat.

2 Using Fabri-Tac, trim the bottom edge of the lampshade with beaded fringe trim. Cover the beaded trim with black trim. Edge the top of the lampshade with the same black trim. Using Quick Grip, embellish the bottom edge of the lampshade with alternating hex nuts and cap nuts.

3 To make a singed fabric rosette, cut a 3¼" circle out of velvet, polyester, and tulle. Cut 2½" circles out of satin, polyester, and tulle.

4 Light the candle and hold the edge of a polyester circle near the flame until it begins to curl. Rotate the fabric until it is singed on all sides.

5 Singe the tulle circles in the same way, rotating the tulle slowly near the flame. Do not singe the velvet or the satin.

6 Layer the circles of fabric largest to smallest in this order: velvet, polyester, tulle, satin, polyester, tulle, and velvet. Top with a shirt button. Sew through all the circles of fabric and the shirt button several times. Repeat to make eight rosettes.

8 On each alternating rosette, pin a bee through a hole in the shirt button.

7 Glue the rosettes around the middle of the lampshade using the Fabri-Tac. Using Quick Grip, glue a coin to every other rosette on top of the button. Top with a watch face, a locking washer, and a rhinestone.

9 Follow the directions on the bottle adapter lamp kit to convert a birdcage (or a candlestick or a bottle) into a lamp. Attach the lampshade to the new lamp base.

10 Make a bundle with old photos, love letters, and other ephemera and bind together with ribbon. Tuck the bundle inside the birdcage. Attach a vintage padlock to the birdcage door with a ribbon scrap tied into a bow.

What once illuminated an underground laboratory now shines as a celebration of extraordinary technologies. The arms of this antiqued chandelier reach out, presenting a reliquary of gears, fuses, and keyholes. Beaded chain spans the distance between each glowing caged bulb encircling an antique padlock that hangs from the center like the pendulum of a long-case clock.

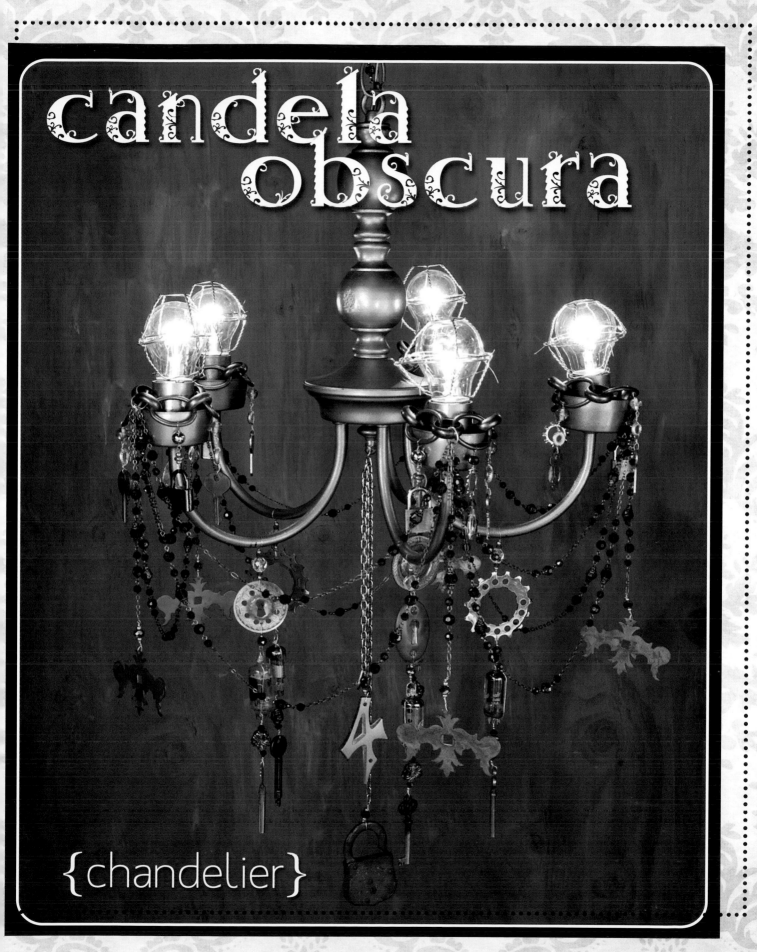

candela obscura

{chandelier}

flea market finds

- ✦ 1 five-arm chandelier
- ✦ 1 vintage padlock
- ✦ 1 house number, brass, 3"
- ✦ 2 bicycle gears, 2⅜"
- ✦ 5 drawer pull plates, brass
- ✦ 10 small keys (luggage, padlock, and mailbox keys)
- ✦ 5 furniture keys, 2¾" to 3"
- ✦ 3 vintage keyholes
- ✦ 5 luggage locks
- ✦ 5 vacuum tubes, 2"
- ✦ 10 champagne cork hoods with cap removed
- ✦ 45" large chandelier chain
- ✦ 17" cuckoo clock chain

materials

- ✦ 5 appliance bulbs, 40-watt
- ✦ 5 external-tooth locking washers, 1"
- ✦ 5 large jump rings, brass, 24mm
- ✦ 16-gauge brass wire
- ✦ 24-gauge wire, brass, copper, and silver finishes
- ✦ Krylon Fusion Textured Shimmer spray paint, Graphite #2521
- ✦ Krylon Outdoor Spaces Hammered Finish spray paint, Brown Metallic #2917
- ✦ Krylon Premium Gold Foil Metallic spray paint, Gold Foil #1050

beads

- ✦ 217" beaded crystal chain, amethyst
- ✦ 6 faceted antique beveled beads, various colors, 5mm
- ✦ 16 faceted crystal rondelles, various colors, 5mm
- ✦ 10 round Venetian glass beads, clear/gold, 10mm
- ✦ 5 faceted round beads, crystal, 12mm
- ✦ 5 round beads, metallic silver finish, 10mm
- ✦ 10 donut beads, brushed gold, 12mm
- ✦ 5 faceted briolettes, crystal, 22mm
- ✦ 10 crystal bicones, red, 6mm
- ✦ 5 Czech pressed-glass flower beads, side-drilled, charcoal, 15mm
- ✦ 37 spacers, copper, 2mm to 6mm
- ✦ 34 pony beads, copper, size 6/0

tools & supplies

- ✦ Round-nose pliers
- ✦ Chain-nose pliers
- ✦ Heavy-duty pliers
- ✦ Wire cutters

putting it together

1 Start by painting the chandelier with a layer of Textured Shimmer Graphite spray paint. To add the look of tarnishing and pitting, spray the chandelier in spots with short bursts of the Hammered Finish Brown Metallic and Gold Foil Metallic spray paints.

2 Encircle each lamp socket with the large chandelier chain to create a bobeche.

3 Make four decorative dangles to hang around each bobeche using small keys, luggage locks, locking washers, and faceted briolettes. Connect the dangles with wrapped loops using any of the 24-gauge wires. Refer to page 15 for instructions to make a wrapped loop.

4 Create large dangles to hang from the five chandelier arms featuring keyholes, bike gears, furniture keys, and vacuum tubes. To hang the vacuum tubes, wrap 24-gauge wire tightly around the top of the tube, down the side, around the bottom pins, and back up the other side. Finish at the top with a wrapped loop.

5 Create swags between each bobeche with 14" and 20" lengths of amethyst beaded chain. Attach with large brass jump rings.

6 Make a dangle to hang from each jump ring with a 7" length of beaded chain. Connect a drawer pull plate to the end of the chain with beads and wrapped loops.

7 Hang the large padlock from 12" of cuckoo clock chain by wiring chain to the center of the chandelier and suspending the lock with beads and wrapped loops. Hang the house number in the same fashion from 7" of cuckoo clock chain.

8 Create lightbulb cages by wiring champagne cork hoods together. Start by snipping the cork hood collar with the wire cutters to remove it.

9 Untwist the wire legs to enlarge the opening for the bulb.

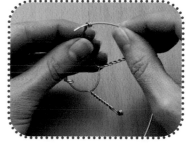

10 Replace the cork hood collar with a 16-gauge wire hoop. Twist the ends of the new hoop together to secure.

11 Fit a bulb through the small opening. Make another modified hood and set it on top.

12 Use short lengths of 24-gauge brass wire to "twist-tie" the cages together. Repeat for all five bulbs.

13 Screw the caged bulbs into the chandelier.

make a switch

You can hang your chandelier in any room of the house even if you don't have a junction box in your ceiling. Just go to a hardware store and ask for a replacement plug to convert your chandelier.

This mystical birdhouse makes time travel possible. Crossing the threshold is a key bearing the message, "Inspiration is granted." One simply needs to pass through the hands of time and enter the portal to take flight.

flying time machine

{birdhouse}

flea market finds

- 3 clock faces, 3" to 4"
- 4 watch faces, ½" to ¾"
- 2 clock gear and axle assemblies, ¾" diameter gear with ½" long axle
- 1 bicycle gear with 1" diameter opening
- 4 flat keys, 1½" to 2"
- 1 furniture key, 2" to 3"
- 8 affiliation pins (i.e., Kiwanis)
- 1 mini compass
- 1 stamped brass tag
- 1 old map
- 1 hardback book, 8½" x 11"
- 1 old paperback book
- 8 shirt buttons

materials

- 1 unfinished wood birdhouse
- 2 Walnut Hollow Creative Metal aluminum sheets, 8½" x 11"
- 2 silver doilies, 4"
- 2 sheets felt, black, 8½" x 11"
- 2 squares of foam core, 2" x 2", ¼" thick
- 1 filigree round, gold, ⅝"
- 1 2-piece hook-and-eye clasp, brass
- 21 Swarovski crystal rhinestones, teal, 4mm
- 4 Swarovski crystal rhinestones, light topaz, 4mm
- 6 star-shaped wheels (Grinding Wheel Dresser Cutters)

- 29 external-tooth locking washers, ½" to ¾"
- 8 wing nuts, ¾"
- 2 washers, brass, 1½"
- 22" chain, gold finish
- 1" chain, copper
- 22-gauge copper wire
- Plaid FolkArt Stains, Oak #2802
- Lisa Pavelka Magic-Glos UV resin

special embellishments

- 2 Vintaj tiny key charms, natural brass, 17mm
- 1 oval frame charm, silver, 35mm
- 1 bee charm
- 1 rhinestone circle charm
- 4 brass stampings, arrows, 80mm
- 4 brass stampings, seashells, 25mm to 35mm

tools & supplies

- Walnut Hollow Creative Metal Mini Tool Set, burnishing tool
- Jolee's Jewels Hotfix Crystal Tool, 3mm tip
- Marvy flower craft punch, 2"
- Beacon Adhesives Quick Grip
- Beacon Adhesives Fabri-Tac
- Foam paintbrush
- Scissors

putting it together

1 Start by the staining the birdhouse with two coats of stain. Let dry between coats.

2 To make the wings, remove the front and back covers of the hardback book. Cut a wing shape out of one of the covers. Lay keys, star-shaped wheels, and bicycle gears on the wing.

3 Cover the wing with a metal sheet. Emboss the metal with the burnishing tool using the nylon universal tip. Be careful not to poke through the metal.

4 Remove the keys, star-shaped wheels, and bicycle gears. Wrap the burnished metal around the wing. Cut a piece of felt to cover the back of the wing and glue down with Fabri-Tac. Repeat to make the opposite wing.

5 Glue the wings to the back of the birdhouse, attaching them with Quick Grip across the eaves. To stabilize the wings, glue two shims of foam core between the wings and the birdhouse.

6 To decorate one side of the roof, glue a silver doily in the center with Quick Grip. Glue on a large clock face, then glue a star-shaped wheel to the center. Add the clock gear assembly. Slip two flat keys over the axle. Arrange the keys to look like clock hands.

7 Embellish the rest of the roof by layering map cutouts and arrows, washers and affiliation pins, and wing nuts. Repeat to decorate the other side of the roof.

8 Adorn the sides of the birdhouse by making flowers using the flower punch and the old map. Layer the center of each bloom with star-shaped wheels, watch faces, and rhinestones. Create stems with the brass seashells. Glue gold chain around the bottom edge of the birdhouse.

9 To decorate the front of the birdhouse, glue the bike gear around the opening to the birdhouse, then glue a piece of gold chain around the opening. Glue a metal tag and a small compass placed on a small filigree round over the door.

10 Embellish the eaves with locking washer and rhinestone florets.

11 Fit a clock face over the perching post at the front, enlarging the hole if needed with a hammer and nail. Decorate it with a bee charm and flank the sides with a 2-piece clasp, one piece on each side.

12 Using pieces of copper chain, attach two tiny key charms from a rhinestone circle charm, then slide it over the post.

13 To make the message key, cut a piece of map to fit in the oval frame charm and glue onto the charm. Cut an interesting phrase from the paperback and glue onto the map. Cover the surface of the oval charm with Magic-Glos resin, then take outside into sunlight to harden for 15 minutes.

14 Wire the message charm onto the furniture key with copper wire. Glue the message key to the front of the birdhouse beneath the clock face.

spread your wings

You can decorate your birdhouse with whatever combination of clock faces, hardware, and vintage finds you like. For inspiration, browse photos of Victorian architecture and gingerbread houses.

Neither snow nor rain nor the haze of wine shall separate these appellations from their designated vessels. Transportation postage stamps from around the globe are tethered to coiled hoops color-coded with beads to match-for an unlabeled potion is poison in the wrong hands.

remember me

{wine charms}

flea market finds

4 mailbox keys, 1¾"
4 vintage postage stamps with common theme in different colors
1 soft leather scrap, dark brown, 4" x 5"

materials

1 piece of clear vinyl, 4" x 5"
4 memory wire earring hoops, brushed silver, 1¼"
16 eyelets, brushed silver, ⅛"
8 hex nuts, brass, ¼"
8 hex nuts, stainless, ¼"
24-gauge silver-plate wire
✦ 24-gauge copper wire

beads

4 faceted crystal rondelles, ruby, 5mm
4 faceted crystal rondelles, topaz, 5mm
4 faceted crystal rondelles, emerald, 5mm
4 faceted crystal rondelles, amethyst, 5mm
4 polka dot glass beads, copper, 5mm
4 Czech pony beads, amber, size 6/o
4 Czech pony beads, clear, size 6/o

tools & supplies

✦ Beacon Adhesives Fabri-Tac
  Leather hole punch, ⅛"
✦ Eyelet tool, ⅛"
✦ Hammer
✦ Scissors
✦ Jeweler's bench block (optional)

putting it together

1 To make the postage stamp tag, cut a 1½" x 2" rectangle out of leather. Cut a piece of clear vinyl the same size. Glue a postage stamp to the center of the leather rectangle and cover with the clear vinyl. To attach the vinyl to the leather, set an eyelet into each corner of the tag using the hammer and the jeweler's bench block.

2 To hang the key, refer to the instructions on page 15 and make a wrapped loop with silver wire through the key. Slide a polka dot bead onto the wire and make a second wrapped loop on the other side of that bead.

3 To create the beaded ring, slide a pony bead onto an earring hoop. Follow with a hex nut, a rondelle, a hex nut, and another rondelle. Next, punch a hole in the center of one side of the tag and slide it onto the ring. Slide on the hanging key. Continue beading the earring hoop with a rondelle, a hex nut, a rondelle, a hex nut, and a pony bead.

4 Hold the tag and beads at the bottom of the earring hoop. Start coiling by laying the wire across the hoop and wrapping the wire tightly once around the hoop.

5 Continue tightly coiling the wire around the hoop until the plain metal side is covered with coiled wire. Repeat for the other side of the hoop.

6 Repeat to make a set of four, each in a different color with added treasures.

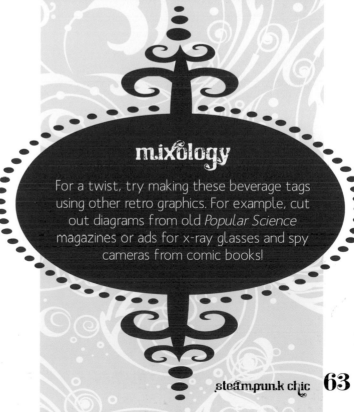

mixology

For a twist, try making these beverage tags using other retro graphics. For example, cut out diagrams from old *Popular Science* magazines or ads for x-ray glasses and spy cameras from comic books!

com·pen·di·um of curiosities

Foolproof crafting is all about having the right materials. While we love to get our vintage keys, padlocks, and watch faces at the flea market, we also need to get some good old retail craft materials. Here are our favorite places to shop when we're not at the swap meet.

BEADS, CHARMS & FINDINGS

Artbeads.com
www.artbeads.com

Baubles & Beads
www.baublesandbeads.com

Beadaholique
www.beadaholique.com

Fire Mountain Gems and Beads
www.firemountaingems.com

Jolee's
www.eksuccessbrands.com

Vintaj Natural Brass Co.
www.vintaj.com

VINTAGE-INSPIRED JEWELRY & SUPPLIES

Cameo Jewelry Supply
www.cameojewelrysupply.com

FDJ On Time
www.fdjtool.com

Victorian Trading Co.
www.victoriantradingco.com

Vintage Jewelry Supplies
www.vintagejewelrysupplies.com

WATCH & CLOCK PARTS

Dave's Watch Parts and Tools
www.daveswatchparts.com

Fire Mountain Gems and Beads
www.firemountaingems.com

Steampunk Supply
www.etsy.com/shop/SteampunkSupply

GENERAL CRAFT SUPPLIES & MATERIALS

Michaels
www.michaels.com

Jo-Ann Fabric and Craft Stores
www.joann.com

Lisa Pavelka
www.lisapavelka.com

Plaid Enterprises
www.plaidcraftexpress.com

Walnut Hollow
www.walnuthollow.com

TOOLS & HARDWARE

Ace Hardware
www.acehardware.com

American Science & Surplus
www.sciplus.com

Widget Supply
www.widgetsupply.com

about the o'neil sisters

Sisters Jennifer and Kitty O'Neil have been crafting together since they were little. They grew up in a house with a Rube Goldberg cartoon garage door opener, a tuba sprouting ostrich feathers, and a carousel horse in the foyer. Their life of collecting and crafting was inevitable!

Ten years ago, the O'Neil sisters decided to quit their day jobs and make a go of it, and they've been working together ever since. With studios in the San Francisco Bay area (and with the cooperation of very understanding husbands), they share their fresh approach to do-it-yourself decorating and crafting in national magazines, on the web, and on their website www.OneilSisters.com.